de la 5e à la 4e

W0204319

The Captain is Missing!

Sylvie ROUCH
écrivain

Caroline CHAPON
enseignante

illustré par

Bruno DAVID

Nathan

Présentation

- **Lire un récit d'aventure en anglais entrecoupé d'exercices de :**
  - compréhension (corrigés à la fin de chaque chapitre).
  - grammaire.

- **S'aider de la traduction :**
  - des mots difficiles signalés par un astérisque* ;
  - des verbes au prétérit irrégulier, soulignés dans le texte (voir la liste page 94).

- **Résoudre des exercices**
  qui permettent de reconstituer l'histoire.

- **Vérifier sa réponse :**
  - elle est juste → suite de l'histoire ;
  - elle est fausse → le corrigé guide pour refaire l'exercice.

- **Consulter le mémento en fin d'ouvrage :**
  il explique la notion abordée dans l'exercice.

- **Regarder la table des matières (p. 92)**
  pour connaître tous les points du programme abordés dans les exercices.

- **Noter les indices sur la dernière page (p. 95) :**
  un par chapitre, ils prouvent que l'enquête avance et que l'histoire est bien comprise.

Coordination éditoriale : Anne-Maty Niang Dagbo
Avec la collaboration de : Magali Corbel
Corrections : Elaine Mc Carthy
Édition : Émilie Million
Maquette couverture et intérieur : Thierry Méléard
Composition : JPM sa
© Nathan, 2009 - ISBN : 978-2-09-186662-8

A Fascinating Shipwreck

1 

My name is Ben and I live in Portsmouth. My parents own a garage there. They both work a lot, especially in the summertime. So they send me away for the holidays. This year I went camping in Cornwall and then, as usual, I went to visit Aunt Sweeny in Saint Peter Port, the capital of Guernsey*.

I spent two amazing weeks there, and right now, I am on a ferryboat in Saint Peter Port harbour*, waving* good-bye to her and to my friends Bill and Betsy.

Guernsey : Guernesey : île située entre l'Angleterre et la France et qui fait partie de l'archipel des îles anglo-normandes
a harbour : un port
wave good bye : dire au revoir d'un signe de la main

Bill and Betsy are thirteen years old, just like me. They are the luckiest twins* in the world because they live in Guernsey all year long. They don't have to go back to England when summer ends*. I hate this moment. I feel so sad. And today, I hate it even more because of the wonderful SMS Betsy sent me a minute ago. Of course, you want to know what she wrote to me but if I tell you now, you won't understand… I must tell you first what happened to the three of us during these holidays…

Que s'est-il passé d'incroyable pendant les vacances de Ben ?

Pour le savoir, coche les deux bonnes réponses.

1 Qui est Ben ?

a. Un jeune habitant de Guernesey qui vient en vacances à Portsmouth. . . . . ☐

b. Un jeune Anglais qui vient en vacances chez sa tante à Guernesey. ☒

2 Qu'est-ce qui le rend triste?

a. Être obligé de rentrer à Portsmouth à la fin des vacances. . . . . ☒

b. Être obligé de passer ses vacances chez sa vieille tante. . . . . ☒

→ **LIS LE CORRIGÉ N° 1 PAGE 14.**

---

twins : des jumeaux
end : se terminer

EXPRIMER L'ABSENCE DE NÉCESSITÉ

Dans la phrase *They <u>don't have to</u> go back to England when summer ends*, que veut dire Ben?

a. Ils ne sont pas obligés de rentrer en Angleterre à la fin des vacances.
b. Ils ne doivent pas rentrer en Angleterre à la fin des vacances, parce que cela leur est interdit.

Tu as répondu a → VA VOIR LE N° 7.
Tu as répondu b → VA VOIR LE N° 5.

mémo I

2

Bravo ! C'est la bonne réponse. Many *s'emploie toujours devant un dénombrable (quelque chose que l'on peut compter) et* much *devant un indénombrable (que l'on ne peut pas compter).*

→ *Tu peux maintenant te rendre au chapitre 2.*

3

Pas si mal ! Tu as en partie raison, mais dans cette phrase, il y a un autre élément qui s'utilise toujours avec le prétérit : c'est ago *qui signifie « il y a ». Il fallait donc répondre : « les deux ! ».*

→ *Va lire la suite de l'histoire au n° 4.*

4

"The Wreck of *The Stella*" is a very old painting. It represents nine seamen*. Eight of them are on a lifeboat*. One is in the sea, drowning* in giant waves. His name is Captain Reeks.

Back home in England, I often think about him. Sometimes I dream that I save his life. And sometimes I dream that I am drowning just like him. It's a horrible dream.

To understand why this painting is so important to me, you must know that I was only six when Tim Bailey, the old museum director, showed it to me for the first time and told me the story of *The Stella*. I still remember our conversation:

"*The Stella* was a beautiful steamer*. The day it wrecked, there were many passengers on board", he said.

"What happened?" I asked.

"Fog*... So much fog that Captain Reeks did not see the rocks", he answered.

---

a seaman : un marin / *seamen* : des marins
a lifeboat : un canot de sauvetage
drown : se noyer
a steamer : un bateau à vapeur
fog : le brouillard

Then I questioned him about the man overboard.
"Did Captain Reeks survive?"
"No, he didn't", he answered.
"What about the passengers?"
"The wreck of *The Stella* took 105 lives", he concluded.

This was the beginning of my fascination for this painting. Every time I came to Guernsey, I went to see "The Wreck of *The Stella*". And every time, I was under spell*.

Now let me come back to what happened in the museum two weeks ago, on the first day of my holidays here. I told you that I was puzzled, right? Well, I was so puzzled that I sat down on a chair and looked at the painting until* I discovered what was wrong.

Then I could not believe my eyes!

under spell : sous le charme
until : jusqu'à ce que

Qu'a remarqué Ben de si étonnant dans son tableau préféré ?

Quel est le nom du tableau préféré de Ben ?

Recopie-le en anglais ci-dessous.

The Wreck of the Stella

C'est ton PREMIER INDICE.

N'oublie pas de le noter sur ta page-indices page 95.

EXPRIMER LA QUANTITÉ

Observe ces 2 phrases :

"The day it wrecked, there were ***many*** *passengers on board."*

"Fog... So ***much*** *fog that Captain Reeks did not see the rocks."*

Quelle est donc d'après toi la règle correcte ?

a. *Many* s'emploie toujours devant un dénombrable (quelque chose que l'on peut compter) et *much* devant un indénombrable (que l'on ne peut pas compter).

b. *Many* s'emploie toujours devant un indénombrable (quelque chose que l'on ne peut pas compter) et *much* devant un dénombrable (que l'on peut compter).

Tu as répondu a → VA VOIR LE N° 2.

Tu as répondu b → VA VOIR LE N° 8.

mémo 5

5

Tu t'es trompé(e) ! Don't have to *exprime l'absence d'obligation et non une interdiction. Pour l'interdiction, tu dois utiliser* mustn't.

→ *Lis le n° 7.*

6

Tu y étais presque ! Mais dans cette phrase, il y a un autre élément qui s'utilise toujours avec le prétérit, c'est la terminaison en -ed *si le verbe est régulier.*

→ *Va au n° 4.*

7

I arrived on this same ferryboat at 5 pm two weeks ago. Aunt Sweeny was waiting for me on the pier*.

"Well, Ben, look at you!" she exclaimed.

"What's wrong with me*?" I asked.

"You are taller than me now!"

"And I am happy to be… You are so small! So how are you, Aunt Sweeny?"

"I'm fine, as usual", she answered.

"And how is the Duke?"

"The Duke can't wait to have tea with you!" Aunt Sweeny said for a joke*.

Hmm… I forgot to tell you that the Duke is a bird, a funny yellow canary, free to go in the house and singing like a pop star.

---

the pier : la jetée
what's wrong with me ? : qu'est-ce que j'ai ?
for a joke : pour blaguer

That evening, I ate a pile of delicious cucumber sandwiches and a piece of carrot cake. My stomach was so big that Aunt Sweeny told me to rest on the sofa. But I could not wait: I ran outside, crossed the street and pushed the door of the most wonderful place in the world.

This place is a museum. I know what you think. You think museums are boring*. Well, this one is NOT because it is very special. You know *Titanic*, of course? Well, this museum honours the memory of unlucky* boats like *Titanic*. There are many paintings there. I love looking at them and my favourite one is called "The Wreck* of *The Stella*". There was nobody in the entry when I arrived so I went into the gallery*. The painting was there, as usual, but when I looked at it, I felt puzzled*. There was something strange about it, but I could not say what...

boring : ennuyeux
unlucky : malchanceux
wreck : faire naufrage / *the wreck* : le naufrage
the gallery : la salle d'exposition
puzzled : intrigué

Qu'y a-t-il de bizarre dans ce tableau ?

Pour le découvrir, coche les 2 bonnes réponses.

1 Quelle phrase marque l'impatience de Ben à se rendre au musée ?

a. I could not wait. .... ☒

b. I felt puzzled. .... ☒

2 Pourquoi Ben aime-t-il tant ce musée ?

a. Parce qu'il peut y voir son tableau préféré. .... ☒

b. Parce qu'il peut y voir des vestiges du *Titanic*. .... ☐

➡ LIS LE CORRIGÉ N° 2 PAGE 14.

RACONTER AU PASSÉ

Dans la phrase *I arrived on this same ferryboat 2 weeks ago*, quel élément prouve que c'est un prétérit simple ?

a. La terminaison du verbe en *-ed*

b. *Ago* à la fin de la phrase

c. Les deux !

Tu as répondu a ➡ VA VOIR LE N° 3.
Tu as répondu b ➡ VA VOIR LE N° 6.
Tu as répondu c ➡ VA VOIR LE N° 13

mémo 2

8

Ce n'est pas la bonne réponse ! Comme tu peux le voir, passengers *est au pluriel. C'est donc un dénombrable. Quant à* fog, *on ne peut pas le compter, puisqu'on ne dit pas 1 brouillard, 2 brouillards... donc c'est un indénombrable.*

→ *À présent, tu peux te rendre au chapitre 2.*

Corrigés des questions de compréhension

1

1. b. Ben est un jeune Anglais qui vient en vacances chez sa tante à Guernesey.

I went to visit Aunt Sweeny in Saint Peter Port, the capital of Guernsey.

2. a. C'est être obligé de rentrer à Portsmouth à la fin des vacances qui le rend triste.

They don't have to go back to England when summer ends.

2

1. a. I could not wait.

I could not wait signifie que Ben dit « Je ne pouvais pas attendre », au sens de « j'en étais incapable ».

2. a. Parce qu'il peut y voir son tableau préféré.

There are many paintings there. I love watching them and my favourite one is called "The Wreck of The Stella".

Mystery at the Museum

1

I recognised the rocks and the sea. I also recognised the lifeboat. So what was the problem?

The problem was that I could not see Captain Reeks. He was NOT in the waves anymore.

Where could he be?

Suddenly I made a crazy wish*. I wished he were safe*. I wished he were on the lifeboat with the other seamen. So I counted them: one, two, three, four, five, six, seven and eight.

---

a wish : un vœu
safe : hors de danger

I counted them again and again but he was not there. Finally, I decided to go and see Tim. His office was upstairs*. It was a messy* room with piles of books everywhere on the floor.

I knocked at the door.

"Come in", said a voice.

I opened the door.

"Good afternoon", said a tall young man. "Who are you?" he asked.

"I am Ben Edison."

"Edison like the scientist?"

"Yes, sir."

"And what can I do for you, Ben Edison?"

"I'm looking for Tim Bailey."

The young man looked surprised.

"Tim Bailey? But he is not here anymore!"

I had a shock: where could he be? Why wasn't he there anymore?

upstairs : à l'étage
messy : en désordre

Qu'est-il arrivé au vieux Tim Bailey, le directeur du musée ?

Quelle erreur Ben relève-t-il dans le tableau ?

Écris en français ce que Ben remarque d'anormal.

C'est ton DEUXIÈME INDICE.

N'oublie pas de le noter sur ta page-indices page 95.

L'ADJECTIF QUALIFICATIF

Pour traduire la phrase « Le jeune homme avait l'air surpris. », je dois écrire :

a. *The* ***young man*** *looked surprised.*
b. *The* ***man young*** *looked surprised.*

Tu as répondu a ➡ VA VOIR LE N° 9.
Tu as répondu b ➡ VA VOIR LE N° 7.

mémo 6

2

Il fallait écrire :

"You are one of his fans, **aren't you?**"

"You are not from Guernsey, **are you?**"

Si tu as répondu correctement, félicitations ! Si tu t'es trompé(e), la règle est facile à retenir ! Souviens-toi :

- *Si l'auxiliaire ou le modal de la phrase est à la forme affirmative, le question-tag sera alors à la forme négative :* "You **are** one of his fans, **aren't** you?"

• *Si l'auxiliaire ou le modal de la phrase est à la forme négative, le question-tag sera à la forme affirmative :* "You **are not** from Guernsey, **are** you?"

→ *Retrouve Ben au n° 4.*

3

Tu t'es trompé(e) ! Le jeune gardien n'y va pas tout seul, car dans cette phrase tu trouves la tournure impérative « Let's + base verbale ». *Cela se traduit par « Allons + base verbale ». En donnant cet ordre, le gardien s'engage également à aller jeter un coup d'œil. Pour te souvenir de ce sens, pense à l'expression* "Let's go" *que tu as sans doute déjà rencontrée.*

→ *Tu peux maintenant aller au n° 6.*

4

Five minutes later, I knocked again. This time, he looked annoyed*.

"What's the problem now?" he asked.

"Something's wrong with a painting, sir."

"Which painting?"

" 'The Wreck of *The Stella*'."

"What's wrong with it?"

"Er… Captain Reeks… He's missing*, sir."

annoyed : agacé
he's missing : il a disparu

"Is this a joke?"
"No, it isn't. Captain Reeks used to be in the waves... And he isn't anymore."
"That is impossible!"
"Impossible... but true*!"
"Let's have a look then", he said.

He followed me downstairs and we entered the gallery. He looked at "The Wreck of *The Stella*", then he looked at me. He was furious.
"Nothing's wrong with this painting, boy. Now go and tell your story to Tim Bailey! He has plenty of time now. Maybe he'll listen to this nonsense*."
I did not reply.
"And don't disturb me again", he shouted before he walked away.
"Go to hell*!" I whispered*.
I did not like this new director: why was he so furious at me? And why was he so busy upstairs?

true : vrai
this nonsense : cette absurdité
go to hell! : va au diable
whisper : chuchoter

Vers qui Ben va-t-il maintenant se tourner pour mener l'enquête ?

Coche les 2 bonnes réponses pour le découvrir...

1 Quelle attitude a le jeune gardien à l'égard de Ben ?

a. Il l'accueille assez froidement puis il est agacé lorsque Ben insiste. . . . . ☐
b. Il est ravi de pouvoir l'aider. ☐

2 Croit-il Ben à propos de la disparition du capitaine Reeks ?

a. Oui, il semble convaincu. . . . . ☐
b. Non, il pense que ce sont des idioties. . . . . ☐

➡ **LIS LE CORRIGÉ N° 2 PAGE 26.**

EXPRIMER LA SUGGESTION

Quand le jeune gardien dit à Ben "*Let's have a look then !*", que veut-il dire ?

a. Il invite Ben à venir jeter un coup d'œil avec lui.
b. Il va jeter un coup d'œil tout seul.

Tu as répondu a ➡ VA VOIR LE N° 6.
Tu as répondu b ➡ VA VOIR LE N° 3.

mémo 8

5 

Bonne réponse, bravo ! Tu peux découvrir la suite de l'énigme au chapitre 3.

6

I wanted to visit Tim Bailey but first, I was anxious* to share my discovery with my friends Bill and Betsy. So I went back to Aunt Sweeny's house and I called the twins. Ten minutes later, they were parking their bicycles in the garden.

This year, Betsy looked a bit different. She looked more like a girl. Her hair was much longer and she was wearing a cotton dress.

“You look really pretty”, I said. She blushed*.

Then I told them about the missing captain on the painting and the new director. Immediately, Betsy had an idea.

“I bet* Tim Bailey did it! I bet he made Captain Reeks disappear”, she said.

“For what reason?” I asked.

“To test the new director”, suggested Bill.

“Tim Bailey is too respectful of the museum to damage* a piece of art”, I protested.

I was anxious to : j'avais hâte de
blush : rougir
I bet : je parie que
damage : dégrader, détériorer

Then Aunt Sweeny opened the front door. The Duke was on her shoulder*.

"Be careful, the Duke... I can hear bees* around here", she said.

It was a joke. A joke about our names, because they all start with a "b", you see...

Then Aunt Sweeny laughed and went in again.

"Maybe Tim Bailey did not exactly damage the painting", Betsy suggested again.

"What do you mean?"

Tim Bailey est-il l'auteur d'une farce ?

Pour le savoir, coche les bonnes réponses.

1 En rentrant du musée, Ben sollicite l'aide :

- **a.** De sa tante Sweeny. . . . . ☐
- **b.** Des jumeaux Betsy et Bill. . . . . ☐

2 Quelle phrase montre que Betsy n'est pas insensible au compliment de Ben ?

- **a.** She blushed. . . . . ☐
- **b.** She had an idea. . . . . ☐

➡ **LIS LE CORRIGÉ N° 3 PAGE 26.**

---

a shoulder : une épaule

a bee : une abeille. En anglais, le mot *bee* se prononce comme la lettre « *b* », ce qui explique le jeu de mots de tante Sweeny.

EXPRIMER L'IMPRESSION

"You ***look*** *really pretty, I said."*

Que signifie le verbe *to look* dans cette phrase ?

a. Quand il est suivi d'un adjectif, le verbe *to look* signifie « avoir l'air ».
b. Quand il est suivi d'un adjectif, le verbe *to look* signifie « regarder ».

Tu as répondu a → Va voir le n° 5.
Tu as répondu b → Va voir le n° 8.

mémo 9

7

En anglais, l'adjectif est toujours DEVANT le nom. Attention ! N'oublie pas qu'il est aussi invariable, c'est-à-dire qu'il ne s'accorde ni en nombre ni en genre avec le nom.

→ *Maintenant, va au n° 9.*

8

Tu n'as pas fait assez attention à l'adjectif qui suit le verbe look ! *Dans la phrase d'exemple, il s'emploie pour exprimer l'impression que Ben a de Betsy. En la regardant, il se rend compte combien elle est jolie. « Regarder » se dit* to look at.

→ *Maintenant que tu as bien compris, tu peux lire la suite de l'énigme au chapitre 3.*

9

I looked around the room. It looked different: no piles of books on the floor… But a new computer on the desk!

"You are one of his fans*", aren't you?

"Yes, I am", I answered.

He smiled. "Tim Bailey retired* last February. I am the new director", he said.

his fans : ses admirateurs
retire : partir en retraite

"I see."
"You are not from Guernsey, are you?"
"No, I am not. I am from Portsmouth."
"Listen. Tim Bailey misses* his young visitors very much… I am sure that he will be very happy to see you."
"But I don't know where he lives", I replied.
"I do!"
The new director <u>wrote</u> down Tim Bailey's address on a piece of paper and <u>gave</u> it to me.
"Thank you, sir", I said.

Then he pushed me out and locked* the door. I wondered why, because Tim Bailey NEVER locked the door…

Y a-t-il un lien entre l'arrivée du nouveau gardien et la disparition du capitaine Reeks ?

Pour le savoir, coche la bonne réponse.

1 Que révèle le jeune gardien à Ben ?

a. Tim Bailey a disparu en février. . . . . ☐
b. Tim Bailey est parti à la retraite en février. . . . . ☐

➡ LIS LE CORRIGÉ N° 1 PAGE 26.

---

miss : regretter
lock : fermer à clé

LES QUESTIONS-TAGS

Complète ces 2 phrases à l'aide de questions-tags :

"You are one of his fans, ____________?"
"You are not from Guernsey, _________?"

➡ VA VOIR LE CORRIGÉ AU N° 2.

mémo 7

Corrigés des questions de compréhension

1

1. b. Tim Bailey est parti à la retraite en février.
Tim Bailey retired last February. Retiens que le verbe *retire* signifie « partir à la retraite ».

2

1. a. Il l'accueille assez froidement puis il est agacé lorsque Ben insiste.
This time, he looked annoyed.

2. b. Non, il pense que ce sont des idioties.
Maybe he'll listen to this nonsense.

3

1. b. Ben sollicite l'aide des jumeaux Betsy et Bill.
I was anxious to share my discovery with my friends Bill and Betsy.

2. a. She blushed.
Le verbe blush *signifie « rougir ».*

3

Tracking Captain Reeks

1

"Maybe he stole the original one and replaced it with another painting", she said.

"A copy?" asked Bill.

"A copy without* Captain Reeks isn't really a copy", I protested. We discussed the matter until late in the evening, so we decided to visit Tim Bailey the day after.

We met at 10am and cycled to Tim Bailey's house. Tim Bailey lived two miles away from Saint Peter Port. He was happy to see us. He invited us to come in and have a glass of orange juice. His house was as messy as his office at the shipwreck

---

without : sans

museum. There were piles of books everywhere on the floor.

I looked at the pictures on the walls but I did not see "The Wreck of *The Stella*".

"It's a pity* you retired!" Bill said.

"I was too old! And I was not qualified..."

"You were more qualified than the new director!" I exclaimed.

"You are wrong*, Ben! This young man studied art in London. He knows a lot!"

"But no one can be as good as you about shipwreck stories", Betsy said.

"Betsy's right! You really are the best", Bill added.

Tim Bailey looked pleased*. "Now stop flattering me, and tell me why you are here", he said.

So I <u>told</u> him about "The Wreck of *The Stella*" and Captain Reeks. Then I told him about the new museum director and his strange behaviour*.

Tim Bailey examined his piles of books for a while* then he <u>took</u> the biggest one out and turned

it's a pity... : c'est dommage que...
you are wrong : tu as tort
pleased : content
the behaviour : le comportement
for a while : pendant quelque temps

the pages until he exclaimed:
"Look at that!"

Tim Bailey va-t-il résoudre le mystère du tableau?

Pour le découvrir, coche la bonne réponse.
Pour quelles raisons Tim Bailey a-t-il quitté le musée ?

a. Il était trop âgé et pas suffisamment qualifié pour le poste. . . . . ☐
b. Il a repris des études d'art à Londres. . . . . ☐

➡ LIS LE CORRIGÉ N° 1 PAGE 39.

EXPRIMER LA COMPARAISON

Pour dire à Tim Bailey qu'il était certainement plus qualifié que le nouveau gardien, quelle tournure Ben utilise-t-il ?

a. *You were **as** qualified **as** the new keeper!*
b. *You were **more** qualified **than** the new keeper!*

Tu as répondu a ➡ VA VOIR LE N° 5.
Tu as répondu b ➡ VA VOIR LE N° 7.

mémo 10

2

Mauvaise réponse. En te référant au mémo n° 4, tu verras que can *peut s'utiliser dans différents cas. Ici,* can *exprime la capacité et non de la permission.*

→ *Pour connaître la suite de l'histoire, va au n° 9.*

3

Félicitations ! Pour dire « faire penser » en anglais, on utilise en effet la structure « make + think *à l'infinitif ».* "It made me think of a painting by Michelangelo." *est donc bien la bonne réponse.*

→ *À présent, va au n° 4.*

4

The brush made a circle in the air then it made the pink angel disappear just like that! We were stupefied.

After saying good-bye, we needed* to relax so we went swimming. Then we cycled back home because it was time for lunch.

We met again at 3 p.m. in front of the most popular Rent-a-car shop* in town. It was called *Easy Driving.*

"Can I help you?" a lady asked.

"We'd like to know if you register* your clients", I said.

"Of course we do!"

"Do you mind if we have a look at the book?"

---

need : avoir besoin de
a Rent-a-car shop : une agence de location de voitures
register : tenir un registre de

"Well... Unless* you have a good reason, it's strictly confidential, you see..."
"We *do* have a good reason", I interrupted and I invented a story. "My uncle had a heart attack during the second week of March", I said. "A man drove him to hospital in a van. It was an *Easy Driving* van. I really want to thank this man because he saved my uncle's life, you see. And I could not do it before. I arrived from Portsmouth yesterday."

The lady looked convinced. "In that case...", she said.

Then she went away for a few minutes and came back with a book.
"Look! A man called Harold Manson rented a van on the 12th. He lives on Hill Road."
"Thank you so much, Madam", we said and we walked out.

Bill looked upset*.
"What's wrong?" I asked.
"This guy can't live on Hill Road", he replied.

---

unless : à moins que
upset : soucieux

Pourquoi Harold Manson ne peut-il pas habiter Hill Road ?

À quel nom la camionnette a-t-elle été louée ?

Écris-le ci-dessous.

C'est ton TROISIÈME INDICE.
N'oublie pas de le noter sur ta page-indices page 95.

INSISTER

"We ***do*** *have a good reason, I interrupted and I made up a story."*

L'auxiliaire *do* sert ici à :

a. Insister sur un fait (« On a vraiment une bonne raison ! »)
b. Répondre simplement (« On a une bonne raison. »)

Tu as répondu a → VA VOIR LE N° 10.
Tu as répondu b → VA VOIR LE N° 8.

5 

Dommage ! Tu as confondu les comparatifs d'égalité et de supériorité. As qualified as *signifie « aussi qualifié que ».* More + *adjectif* + than *(ou un adjectif court se terminant par* -er*) s'utilise pour comparer 2 choses et exprimer la supériorité (Plus…que).*

→ *Lis le n° 7.*

6

*Tu t'es trompé(e)! Pour dire «faire penser» en anglais, tu dois utiliser la structure «*make + *infinitif».* "I thought of a painting by Michelangelo" *signifie «je pensais à une peinture de Michel-Ange».*

→ *Va au n° 4.*

7

It was a black and white reproduction of "The Wreck of *the Stella*". The photo was small, but we could clearly see Captain Reeks in the waves. I clapped my hands with excitement.

"Don't be too enthusiastic, Ben. This picture does not prove anything", Tim said.

"Yes, it does! It proves that Captain Reeks exists on the original painting", I replied.

"No it doesn't! There is no proof* that the original painting is the one in the photo."

"YOU can prove it!"

"I am not in charge of the museum anymore, kids! I can't investigate* this!"

"Come on, Tim… Help us… Please!"

"Why don't you go and see Chester Fog?"

---

no proof : aucune preuve
investigate : mener une enquête

"Who is Chester Fog?"

"He's a talented painter. Occasionally, he restores paintings, too. A month before I retired, I sent him "The Wreck of *The Stella*". He was supposed to clean it and brighten* the colours… He might help you."

"Where does he live?"

"Near Ladies' Bay. But be careful! The man can be rude*, and he doesn't like to be disturbed."

Le peintre va-t-il accepter de les recevoir ?

Coche les bonnes réponses pour le savoir.

1 Qu'y a-t-il dans le livre de Tim Bailey ?

a. Une reproduction du *Naufrage du Stella* montrant le capitaine Reeks en train de se noyer. . . . . ☐
b. Une reproduction du *Naufrage du Stella* sans aucune trace du capitaine Reeks. . . . . ☐

2 Pourquoi le peintre Chester Fog peut-il les aider ?

a. Il a peint *Le Naufrage du Stella*. . . . . ☐
b. Il a restauré *Le Naufrage du Stella*. . . . . ☐

→ LIS LE CORRIGÉ N° 2 PAGE 39.

brighten : raviver
rude : grossier

EXPRIMER LA CAPACITÉ

"You can prove it!"

Ben dit à Tim :

a. Qu'il peut le prouver (qu'il en a la capacité, les facultés).
b. Qu'il l'autorise à le prouver.

Tu as répondu a → VA VOIR LE N° 9.
Tu as répondu b → VA VOIR LE N° 2.

mémo 4

8

Mauvaise réponse! En anglais, pour insister sur ce que l'on dit, on fait précéder le verbe de l'auxiliaire do, does *ou* did *selon le temps de la phrase.*

→ *Si tu as bien tout compris, va vite au chapitre 4!*

9

Half an hour later, we were there.

Chester Fog was at work. He was painting an angel dancing in a blue sky. It made me think of a painting by Michelangelo*.

"What do you want?" he asked.

"Do you remember restoring a shipwreck painting called 'The Wreck of *The Stella*'?" I asked.

"Of course I do", he said.

Michelangelo : Michel-Ange (peintre italien de la Renaissance, célèbre pour avoir peint des anges au plafond de la chapelle Sixtine, au Vatican).

"Do you remember this painting *precisely*?" Betsy asked.

"I restore too many paintings to remember *all* of them precisely", he replied.

Then he took his brush* and put a large touch of pink on the angel's back.

"When did you finish restoring it?" I asked.

He looked at a calendar on the wall and replied: "Second week of March."

"Did you bring it back to the museum?" Bill asked.

"No, I didn't. A delivery man* came for it. He had a pigtail*."

"Do you remember anything else about him?"

"No, except he was driving a rented van*", he added.

For a few seconds, he looked at his painting and all of a sudden, he raised his brush as if it were a sword* and, and…

---

his brush : son pinceau
a delivery man : un coursier
a pigtail : une queue de cheval
a rented van : une camionnette de location
a sword : une épée

Chester Fog est-il dangereux ?

Pour le découvrir, coche les bonnes réponses.

1 Que dit Chester Fog à ses visiteurs ?

a. Qu'après avoir restauré le tableau, il l'a rapporté au musée des Épaves. . . . . ☐

b. Qu'un livreur avec une queue de cheval est venu chez lui et a emporté le tableau. . . . . ☐

2 Quel élément complémentaire leur permet d'avancer dans leur enquête ?

a. Le livreur conduisait une camionnette de location. . . . ☐

b. Le livreur conduisait une camionnette bleue. . . . . . ☐

→ **LIS LE CORRIGÉ N° 3 PAGE 39.**

FAIRE FAIRE

« Cela me faisait penser à une peinture de Michel-Ange » dit Ben en parlant du travail de Chester Fog.

Quelle est la bonne traduction ?

a. *"I thought of a painting by Michelangelo."*

b. *"It made me think of a painting by Michelangelo."*

Tu as répondu a → **VA VOIR LE N° 6.**

Tu as répondu b → **VA VOIR LE N° 3.**

mémo 11

10 

Bravo ! L'auxiliaire do *sert en effet à insister sur un fait.*

→ *Va vite au chapitre 4 pour connaître la suite des aventures de Ben, Bill et Betsy.*

Corrigés des questions de compréhension

1

1. a. Il était trop âgé et pas suffisamment qualifié pour le poste.
I was too old! And I was not qualified…

2

1. a. Une reproduction du *Naufrage du Stella* montrant le capitaine Reeks en train de se noyer.
The photo was small but we could clearly see Captain Reeks in the waves.

2. b. Il a restauré *Le Naufrage du Stella.*
He was supposed to clean it and brighten the colours…

3

1. b. Chester Fog dit qu'un livreur avec une queue de cheval est venu chez lui et a emporté le tableau.
A delivery man came over… He had a pigtail.

2. a. Le livreur conduisait une camionnette de location.
He was driving a rented van.

4

A Strange Coincidence

1

"Why not?"

"Because Hill Road is a deserted road, somewhere in the south. There are no houses over there."

"Not even a farm?" I asked.

"Nothing except a manor."

"Then I suppose that Harold Manson lives in this manor!"

"Impossible", Bill replied.

"Unless he is a ghost*", Betsy added.

"What are you talking about? You are not serious, are you?"

a ghost : un fantôme

"Yes, we are! This manor is not an ordinary manor."

"What's so special about it?"

"It's haunted*", Ben!

"Wahoo! And what is it called?"

"Haunted Manor!" they replied.

And they laughed until Betsy suddenly turned pale and started to tremble.

"What's wrong with you, Betsy? Aren't you feeling well?" Bill asked.

Pourquoi Betsy frissonne-t-elle de peur ?

Pour le savoir, coche les bonnes réponses.

1 Que trouve-t-on à Hill Road ?

a. Une ferme. . . . . ☐
b. Un manoir. . . . . ☐

2 Quelle est la particularité du manoir ?

a. C'est un manoir abandonné qui a la réputation d'être hanté. . . . . ☐
b. C'est un joli manoir que les touristes peuvent visiter. . . . . ☐

➡ **LIS LE CORRIGÉ N° 1 PAGE 48.**

haunted : hanté

NO ET SES COMPOSÉS

Dans la phrase *"There are no houses over there"*,
par quelle expression peut-on remplacer "*There are no houses*"?

a. *There aren't any houses.*
b. *There are some houses.*

Tu as répondu a → VA VOIR LE N° 6.
Tu as répondu b → VA VOIR LE N° 5.

mémo 12

2

Au contraire ! Betsy n'est pas du tout sûre qu'il soit un fantôme. C'est pourquoi elle utilise might *qui exprime l'incertitude et le doute. Tu peux revoir ce point en consultant le mémo n° 13.*

→ *Va au n° 4.*

3

Bravo !

→ *Lis vite la suite de l'énigme au chapitre 5.*

4

The Manor was not welcoming: there was a high wall around its garden and there were spikes* on top of its gates*. We left our bicycles behind a

---

spikes : des piques
gates : grilles d'entrée

tree and walked around until we could find a place easy to climb*. When we jumped down on the other side, we discovered that the garden looked like a jungle.

"Where is the Manor?" Betsy asked.

"It's over there, look!" Bill replied.

We started to follow* him but the grass was so high that it was difficult to walk.

"Are you OK?" I asked Betsy.

"No, I am not… I am afraid of snakes*. Aren't you afraid of snakes?" she asked.

I pretended I was not.

"Would you feel better if I held your hand*?" I asked.

"Yes, I would", she replied.

So I took her hand and she felt better. I felt really good too, until my right foot bumped* into something hard.

What was it? A coffin*?

---

climb : escalader
follow : suivre
snakes : des serpents
if I held your hand : si je te tenais par la main
bump into : heurter
a coffin : un cercueil

Sur quel obstacle Ben et Betsy ont-ils soudain trébuché ?

Pour le découvrir avec eux, coche la bonne réponse.

1 Comment les trois amis pénètrent-ils dans le parc de Haunted Manor ?

a. Ils trouvent le portail ouvert et entrent. . . . . ☐
b. Ils escaladent le mur qui protège la propriété. . . . . ☐

2 Pourquoi Ben prend-il la main de Betsy ?

a. Parce qu'elle a peur des serpents. . . . . ☐
b. Parce qu'elle a peur de se perdre dans les hautes herbes. . . . . ☐

→ **LIS LE CORRIGÉ N° 2 PAGE 48.**

EXPRIMER LE CONDITIONNEL

Comment traduire « Te sentirais-tu mieux si je te tenais la main ? » :

a. *“ **Would** you feel better if I **held** your hand?”*
b. *“ **Will** you feel better if I **hold** your hand?”*

Tu as répondu a → VA VOIR LE N° 3.
Tu as répondu b → VA VOIR LE N° 7.

mémo 14

5 

Tu t'es trompé(e) ! Some *ne s'emploie que dans les phrases affirmatives, sauf dans le cas d'une demande polie. Ex. :* Would you like some water?
Any *en revanche s'utilise dans les phrases interrogatives ou négatives.* → *Va au n° 6.*

6

"The man who rented the van, this Harold Manson…", she whispered.

"What about him?"

"Think of his initials… They are like the initials of Haunted Manor", she whispered again.

"So what?" Bill asked.

"So he might be a GHOST", she said.

"Don't tell me you believe* in ghosts! Nobody believes in ghosts nowadays*!" Bill replied.

Then he started to move his arms over his head and shout "Hoo, hoo" to make fun of her*. Betsy was furious.

"Aunt Sweeny does. She believes that the Duke is somebody's ghost", I said to make her feel better.

"Does she?"

"Yes, she does!"

Betsy smiled at me.

A few minutes later, the three of us were cycling south. The road was not good and cycling was not easy. I must admit that I was not feeling very com-

believe : croire
nowadays : de nos jours
to make fun of her : pour se moquer d'elle

fortable. I was puzzled* by this coincidence of initials. What was the link* between Harold Manson and Haunted Manor? Did the letters "H.M." correspond to some secret code?

Quelle étrange coïncidence lie Harold Manson au manoir de Hill Road ?

Que pense Betsy à propos d'Harold Manson ?

Écris ta réponse ci-dessous.

C'est ton QUATRIÈME INDICE.

N'oubliez pas de le noter sur ta page-indices page 95.

EXPRIMER LA PROBABILITÉ, L'ÉVENTUALITÉ

Quand Betsy dit : *"He **might be** a sort of ghost"*,

elle exprime son sentiment :

a. Avec certitude.
b. Avec incertitude.

Tu as répondu a → Va voir le n° 2.
Tu as répondu b → Va voir le n° 4.

mémo 13

---

puzzled : intrigué
the link : le rapport

7

C'est faux ! Tu dois retenir que will *est l'auxiliaire du futur (Te sentir***as***-tu mieux si je te tiens la main?) et* would *celui du conditionnel. Consulte pour t'aider le mémo n° 14.*

→ *Va vite lire le chapitre 5.*

Corrigés des questions de compréhension

1

1. b. Un manoir.
Nothing except a manor.

2. a. C'est un manoir abandonné qui a la réputation d'être hanté.
"What's so special about it?" "It's haunted, Ben!"

2

1. b. Ils escaladent le mur qui protège la propriété.
(We) walked around until we could find a place easy to climb.

2. a. Ben prend la main de Betsy parce qu'elle a peur des serpents.
I am afraid of snakes.

A Secret Tunnel

1

It was not a coffin. It was a metal ring* and it was fixed to a round piece of wood. Bill helped me push it away… and guess what! The piece of wood covered a hole*!

"I bet it is a secret passage", Bill said.

"What if it has lots of rats and skeletons?" Betsy exclaimed.

"You are really too imaginative! It's only a hole", Bill replied.

---

a ring : un anneau
a hole : un trou

"But don't forget the rumours..."

"What rumours?" I asked.

"We'd better not* tell you now or you would run away", she replied.

Then we inspected the hole. Suddenly Bill noticed a ladder*. It looked like the ladders you could see on boats, in the harbour.

"Let's go down there", he said.

"Now?"

"Of course, now!" said Bill.

"But we need a torch*!" Betsy protested.

"She is right. Let's go home and come back tonight with a torch", I suggested.

So we pushed the piece of wood back. At the same time, we heard a terrible noise coming from the hole. It sounded like a door creaking*. We were terrified.

"Now it's time to tell me what you know about this place!" I told the twins.

---

we'd better not tell you now or... : mieux vaut ne rien te dire maintenant sinon...
a ladder : une échelle
a torch : une lampe de poche
a door creaking : une porte qui grince

Quel secret les jumeaux vont-ils révéler à Ben ?

Pour le savoir, réponds aux questions suivantes.

Que cache le couvercle en bois ?

C'est ton CINQUIÈME INDICE.

N'oublie pas de le noter sur ta page-indices page 95.

1 Ben, Betsy et Bill explorent-ils le passage secret ?

a. Non, ils décident de revenir à la nuit tombée. .... ☐

b. Oui, ils l'explorent immédiatement. .... ☐

2 La phrase *"It sounded like a door creaking"* signifie que :

a. Le bruit leur faisait penser à une porte qui grince. ... ☐

b. La trappe s'est refermée sur eux. .... ☐

→ LIS LE CORRIGÉ N° 1 PAGE 58.

EXPRIMER UN CONSEIL

Dans laquelle de ces deux phrases Betsy donne-t-elle un conseil ?

a. *"Whaf if it has lots of rats and skeletons?"*

b. *"We'd better not tell you or you'll run away."*

Tu as répondu a → VA VOIR LE N° 4.

Tu as répondu b → VA VOIR LE N° 6.

2

Tu as sans doute été troublé(e) par le 's *qui, après le sujet, peut faire penser à l'auxiliaire* be *conjugué au présent. Mais regarde ce qui suit : ce n'est pas un adjectif mais un nom. Tante Sweeny ne peut pas être un garage !*
→ *Revois le cas possessif en t'aidant du mémo n° 15, puis va au n° 3.*

3

"A roar*?! What if we meet tigers?" Betsy exclaimed.
"Stop imagining things! There aren't any tigers here", Bill answered.
"Not even tigers escaped from a zoo?" I suggested.
"The closest zoo is in Jersey. Tigers will not swim so far", he said with a touch of irony.

I smiled but I still felt nervous.
"I suggest you and Betsy inspect this part of the tunnel while I inspect the other part", he said again.
"I don't want you to be alone", Betsy protested.
"Don't worry. I will be OK", he replied.
"Let's meet outside in fifteen minutes!" I suggested.

We watched Ben go, then we started to explore our part of the tunnel. As we advanced, the roar

---

a roar : un rugissement

was louder and louder*. Suddenly, we arrived at a cave*. We could feel fresh air coming in from… the ocean!

The noise… That was it, of course… It was the roar of the ocean!

We felt better but we were still a little bit nervous. “This place looks abandoned like an old pirates’ nest*!” I said.

“Not so abandoned, look!” Betsy exclaimed.

And she pointed to some prints* on the sand…

Qui a pu laisser ces empreintes dans le sable ?

Pour le découvrir, coche les bonnes réponses.

1 Une fois dans le tunnel, Ben et Betsy entendent un grondement. D’où provient-il ?

a. D’un tigre échappé d’un zoo. . . . . ☐
b. Du bruit des vagues sur les rochers. . . . . ☐

2 Pourquoi, selon Betsy, ce lieu n’est-il pas abandonné?

a. Parce qu’elle entend des voix. . . . . ☐
b. Parce qu’elle a vu des empreintes sur le sable. . . . . ☐

→ **LIS LE CORRIGÉ N° 3 PAGE 58.**

louder and louder : de plus en plus fort
a cave : une grotte
a pirates’ nest : un repaire de pirates
prints : des empreintes

ARRÊTER DE FAIRE QUELQUE CHOSE

Stop imagining things! **signifie :**

a. « Arrête-toi et imagine des choses ! »
b. « Arrête d'imaginer des choses ! »

Tu as répondu a → VA VOIR LE N° 7.
Tu as répondu b → VA VOIR LE N° 5.

mémo 16

4

Tu t'es trompé(e) ! What if, *qui signifie « et si... ? », exprime la supposition et non le conseil, illustré dans cette phrase par la tournure* had better. **"We'd better** not tell you or you'll run away" *se traduit par « Il ne **vaut mieux** pas que l'on te le dise sinon tu partirais en courant ! »*

→ *Va au n° 6.*

5

Bonne réponse !

→ *Rends-toi vite au chapitre 6.*

6

"A hundred years ago, a young man lived here. His name was Lord Oliver Remington", said Betsy while we were cycling back home.

"He was brilliant. He was rich too", Bill continued.

"And what happened to him?"

"He was poisoned..."

"Wahoo!"

"The criminal was never arrested and nobody wanted to live in the Manor after the crime", Bill said.

"Nobody... except the Lord's ghost!" Betsy concluded.

Before going to bed that evening, I took a torch from Aunt Sweeny's garage and I put it in my backpack*.

When Aunt Sweeny was asleep, I got dressed again. And at midnight, I walked out and met the twins outside. Bill had a torch too.

We cycled to the Manor again. We jumped over the wall, then we pushed the piece of wood away and climbed down the ladder. We counted 25 steps before we reached the ground*.

Then we walked along a tunnel. Suddenly the passage divided and there were two ways to go.

"Listen", said Bill.

"What?"

"Can't you hear a noise?"

---

a backpack : un sac à dos
the ground : le sol

He was right. There was a noise. It was distant and it sounded like…

Quelle est la cause de ce bruit lointain ?

Pour le savoir, coche les bonnes réponses.

1 Qu'est-il arrivé à Lord Oliver Remington ?

a. Il a été empoisonné. .... ☐
b. La police l'a arrêté parce que c'était un criminel. ... ☐

2 Pourquoi Ben attend-il que tante Sweeny s'endorme ?

a. Pour l'empoisonner. .... ☐
b. Pour retourner explorer le passage secret. .... ☐

➡ **LIS LE CORRIGÉ N° 2 PAGE 58.**

LE CAS POSSESSIF

À quoi sert le *'s* dans la phrase : *"Aunt Sweeny's garage"*?

a. Signifier que le garage appartient à tante Sweeny.
b. C'est le verbe *be* conjugué au présent.

Tu as répondu a ➡ VA VOIR LE N° 3.
Tu as répondu b ➡ VA VOIR LE N° 2.

7 

Tu t'es trompé(e) ! Stop imagin**ing** things *exprime la fin et non le début d'une action. Cela est marqué par le verbe à la forme* -ing. *Pour t'en souvenir, pense par*

exemple à ton professeur : tu as dû l'entendre dire au début d'un cours "Stop talking!".

→ *Maintenant, va vite découvrir la suite de l'énigme au chapitre 6.*

Corrigés des questions de compréhension

1

1. a. Ils décident de revenir à la nuit tombée.
Let's go home and come back tonight with a torch.

2. a. Le bruit leur faisait penser à une porte qui grince.
Le verbe *creak* exprime un son sec, qui se traduit par « grincer ».

2

1. a. Il a été empoisonné.
He was poisoned…

2. b. Pour retourner explorer le passage secret.
We cycled to the Manor again. We jumped over the wall, then we pushed the piece of wood away and climbed down the ladder.

3

1. b. Ce bruit provient du bruit des vagues sur les rochers.
It was the roar of the ocean!

2. b. Parce qu'elle a vu des empreintes sur le sable.
And she pointed to some prints on the sand.

Spies at Haunted Manor

1 

"Our ghost is wearing sports shoes, isn't he?" I said for a joke.

Then we followed the prints. We soon reached a cove* in the open air. The cove was protected by rocks. A luxurious yacht was anchored* there. The cabin was lighted by a torch and a man was moving inside. He was on the point of sailing away*.

"There's our man", I said.

"But which one? Harold Manson or Lord Oliver Remington's ghost?" Betsy asked.

a cove : une crique
anchored : à l'ancre
sail away : partir en voilier

"What if the two were only one?" I replied.

She smiled at me and it was MAGIC! She looked so beautiful in the moonlight*... Time to kiss her or to whisper "I love you", I thought.

But I did not kiss her. And I did not say a word. (Umm... Next year I will. I promise I will!)

Then the man walked out of the cabin. The first thing I noticed* was that he did not have a pigtail.

The second thing I noticed was that...

"Do you recognize him?" Betsy asked.

"Yes, I do! What the hell* is HE doing on this yacht?"

Qui Ben et Betsy reconnaissent-ils sur le yacht ?

Pour le savoir, coche les bonnes réponses.

1 Que font Ben et Betsy une fois dans la grotte ?

a. Ils font demi-tour parce que c'est l'heure de retrouver Bill. . . . . ☐

b. Ils suivent les traces de pas et se retrouvent devant une crique. . . . . ☐

---

in the moonlight : au clair de lune
notice : remarquer
What the hell is HE doing on this yacht ? : Nom d'un chien, mais qu'est-ce qu'il fabrique sur ce yacht ?

2 Que découvrent-ils ?

a. Une chaussure appartenant à Bill. . . . . ☐
b. Un yacht visiblement sur le point de lever l'ancre. . ☐

➡ **LIS LE CORRIGÉ N° 1 PAGE 67.**

S'EXPRIMER AU PASSIF

Comment traduis-tu en français la phrase : "*The cove was protected by rocks*" ?

a. « La crique **est protégée** par des rochers »
b. « La crique **était protégée** par des rochers »

Tu as répondu a ➡ VA VOIR LE N° 5.
Tu as répondu b ➡ VA VOIR LE N° 6.

mémo 17

2

Attention ! L'auxiliaire do *ne s'utilise qu'au présent simple.*

→ *Va au n° 4.*

3

Bravo ! Tu peux à présent lire le chapitre 7.

4

Betsy wanted me to go back to Saint Peter Port and tell the police. I did not think it was a good idea. The police will not believe a word of the story, I thought.
"Maybe, Bill had an accident. Maybe he twisted

his ankle*. I must go back there", I said.
"What if you disappear too?" asked Betty.
"If we are not here in half an hour, go back home and tell your parents!"

I switched my torch on again and left. This time, when the tunnel parted, I went the other way. Five minutes later, I arrived in front of a door. I tried to open it but it was locked. I had to go back.
"I did not find Bill but I know where he is", I told Betsy.
"Where is he?"

I pointed out the Manor to her. We observed it silently and suddenly, our eyes were attracted by the flash of a light.
"Did you see that light?" I asked.
"Yes, I did… Let's go to the manor", she replied.

Ben et Betsy vont-ils parvenir à entrer dans le manoir ?

Pour le savoir, réponds aux questions suivantes :

1 Que décide Ben ?

a. De redescendre dans le tunnel. .... ☐
b. D'aller prévenir la police. .... ☐

➡ **LIS LE CORRIGÉ N° 3 PAGE 67.**

to twist one's ankle : se fouler la cheville

2 Quel élément prouve qu'il y a quelqu'un dans le manoir ?

Inscris-le ci-dessous.

C'est ton SIXIÈME INDICE.

N'oublie pas de le noter sur ta page-indices page 95.

EXPRIMER LA SUPPOSITION

Comment dirais-tu « Peut-être que Bill a eu un accident. » ?

a. "Bill probably had an accident." . . . . ☐
b. "Maybe Bill had an accident." . . . . ☐

Tu as répondu a → VA VOIR LE N° 7.
Tu as répondu b → VA VOIR LE N° 3.

mémo 13

5

Tu t'es trompé(e) ! N'oublie pas la construction de la forme passive : sujet + be *que l'on conjugue au temps de la forme active + participe passé. La phrase* "The cove **was protected** by rocks" *est au passé, comme le prouve* was. *On traduit donc en français par « La crique **était** protégée par des rochers. »*

→ *Revois le passif grâce au mémo n° 17 puis va lire le n° 6.*

6

"I don't know but look! It's time to go back and meet Bill", I answered.

We arrived first on top of the hole. We sat down in the grass to wait for Bill. We were anxious* to hear his story. And we were anxious to tell him about the cove, and the yacht, and the mysterious presence of Chester Fog on that yacht!

What was the painter doing there? Did he tell us the truth* about "The Wreck of The Stella"? Did Harold Manson really exist? If so, where was he? We could not answer any of these questions.

At one o'clock in the morning, we started to worry* about Bill.

At two o' clock, he was still missing* and Betsy was in a real panic.

Why didn't he come back? Was he trapped*? Was he hurt?

---

we were anxious to : on avait hâte de
the truth : la vérité
worry : s'inquiéter
he was still missing : il n'était toujours pas revenu
trapped : tombé dans un piège

Qu'est-il arrivé à Bill ?

Pour le savoir, coche les bonnes réponses.

1 Pourquoi Ben et Betsy sont-ils impatients de retrouver Bill ?

a. Pour lui dire qu'ils ont rencontré Harold Manson. . . ☐
b. Pour lui dire qu'ils ont vu Chester Fog sur un yacht. ☐

2 Pourquoi Bill ne remonte-t-il pas du souterrain ?

a. D'après Ben, il se serait perdu. . . . . ☐
b. D'après Ben, il serait tombé dans un piège ou il se serait blessé. . . . . ☐

➡ LIS LE CORRIGÉ N° 2 PAGE 67.

S'EXPRIMER AU PASSÉ

Pour poser une question au prétérit simple, que doit-on utiliser ?

a. L'auxiliaire *do* + sujet + verbe ?
b. L'auxiliaire *did* + sujet + verbe ?

Tu as répondu a ➡ VA VOIR LE N° 2.
Tu as répondu b ➡ VA VOIR LE N° 4.

mémo 2

7

Probably *ne te fait-il pas penser à un mot français? Cela veut dire « probablement » ! Pour dire « Peut-être que Bill a eu un accident », on emploie* maybe *qui signifie « peut-être ».*

→ *Si tu as bien compris la différence, va lire le chapitre 7.*

Corrigés des questions de compréhension

1

1. b. Ils suivent les traces de pas et se retrouvent devant une crique.
Then we followed the prints. We soon reached a cove.

2. b. Un yacht visiblement sur le point de lever l'ancre.
A luxurious yacht was anchored there. He was on the point of sailing away.

2

1. b. Pour lui dire qu'ils ont vu Chester Fog sur un yacht.
We were anxious to tell him about the cove, and the yacht, and the mysterious presence of Chester Fog on that yacht!

2. b. D'après Ben, il serait tombé dans un piège ou il se serait blessé.
Was he trapped? Was he hurt?

3

1. a. Ben décide de redescendre dans le tunnel.
I must go back there.

7

Trapped!

1

We approached one of the windows and we tried to look inside. But it was dark and we could not see anything.

Suddenly we heard the noise of a fight*. Then we recognized the voice of Chester Fog. He was furious.

"What are you doing here in the middle of the night?"

"I'm... I'm looking for ghosts, sir", Bill answered.

"Looking for ghosts? Don't lie* to me, boy! You are looking for trouble*. That's what you are looking for!"

a fight : une bagarre
don't lie to me! : ne me raconte pas d'histoires !
you're looking for trouble : tu cherches des ennuis

"Please, believe me. I came here because of the rumours."

"What rumours?"

"The rumours about Haunted Manor!"

"What about your nosy* friends? Are they here with you?"

"No, sir. They… They are in bed… They are asleep… I came alone."

"And how did you get in, you nasty little spy*?"

"Through a window. It was open. Now please, let me go away… I promise I won't say a word!"

"Shut up and follow me!"

"Where are we going?"

"YOU are not going anywhere, young man!" the painter replied.

Betsy hugged* me. She was trembling.

"Bill is in danger. Let's go!" I said.

We ran away and cycled back to Saint Peter Port as fast as we could.

---

nosy : qui se mêle de ce qui ne le regarde pas
nasty little spy : sale petit espion
hug : serrer dans ses bras

Ben et Betsy vont-ils réussir à revenir à temps pour sauver Bill ?

Pour le savoir, coche les 2 bonnes réponses.

1 Qu'entendent Ben et Betsy ?

a. Un appel à l'aide. .... ☐
b. Une bagarre. .... ☐

2 Chester Fog a-t-il l'intention d'emmener Bill avec lui sur son yacht ?

a. Oui, il dit qu'il va l'emmener et le séquestrer à bord. ☐
b. Non, il lui dit qu'il n'ira nulle part. .... ☐

→ LIS LE CORRIGÉ N° 1 PAGE 78.

S'EXPRIMER AU PRÉSENT PROGRESSIF

*"What **are** you **doing** here in the middle of the night?"*
*"I **am looking** for ghosts!"*

Que signifie la structure *be* + verbe à la forme *-ing*?

a. L'action est en train de se passer. .... ☐
b. C'est une action habituelle. .... ☐

Tu as répondu a → VA VOIR LE N° 6.
Tu as répondu b → VA VOIR LE N° 4.

mémo 3

2

Mauvaise réponse ! Tu dois retenir que may *s'emploie pour demander une autorisation ou une permission dans une langue assez soutenue. Pour un registre un peu plus familier, on utilisera plutôt* can.

→ *Va au n°3.*

3

He was not hurt* but he was shocked. He sat down between Betsy and me and told us his story. "There was a door at the end of the passage", he said.

"Wasn't it locked?" I asked.

"No, and I walked into a room. It looked like Ali Baba's cave. There were tons of things everywhere!"

"Like what?"

"Like china*, bronze, antiques..."

"Any oil paintings?"

"Lots of oil paintings!"

"Did you see "The Wreck of *The Stella*"?" Betsy asked.

"I did... Tim Bailey said that Chester Fog was a good painter, didn't he?"

"Yes, he did!"

"Well, he forgot to tell us that he was a trafficker too!"

"And a forger*?"

---

hurt : blessé
china : de la porcelaine
a forger : un faussaire

"And a forger!"

"Why didn't you come back on time*?" I asked.

"I couldn't!" The door closed behind me and I could not open it again. Then I discovered that I was under the Manor, so I decided to explore it...

"That is when Chester Fog caught you!"

"That's right!"

"What happened after that?"

"He locked me in a closet* and he left." 'This is the end', I thought. 'Nobody will find me here except rats!'

"Look!" Betsy exclaimed.

A group of men were coming back. As they passed by the car, we recognized Chester Fog. He was wearing handcuffs*...

Les ennuis sont-ils terminés pour Ben, Bill et Betsy ?

1 Après sa libération, que révèle Bill à ses amis ?

a. Qu'il a retrouvé *Le Naufrage du Stella* parmi d'autres objets de valeur dans le souterrain. . . . . ☐

b. Qu'il n'a pas retrouvé *Le Naufrage du Stella* dans le souterrain. . . . . ☐

➡ LIS LE CORRIGÉ N° 3 PAGE 78.

---

on time : à temps
a closet : un placard
handcuffs : des menottes

2 Quelle phrase prouve que Chester Fog a été arrêté ?

Recopie-la en anglais ci-dessous.

C'est ton SEPTIÈME INDICE.

N'oublie pas de le noter sur ta page-indices page 95.

S'EXPRIMER AU FUTUR

« Personne ne me **trouvera** jamais. » pense Bill enfermé dans le manoir.

Comment traduire sa réflexion ?

- **a.** *"Nobody* ***would*** *ever find me."* . . . . ☐
- **b.** *"Nobody* ***will*** *ever find me."* . . . . ☐

Tu as répondu a → VA VOIR LE N° 7.

Tu as répondu b → VA VOIR LE N° 5.

mémo 14

4 

Tu t'es trompé(e) ! Tu as confondu le présent simple et le présent progressif (be + -ing). *Le présent simple exprime une action habituelle, une caractéristique (ex. :* I play tennis every Saturday *: je joue au tennis tous les samedis). En revanche, le présent progressif s'utilise pour dire qu'une action est en cours au moment où l'on parle.*

→ *Découvre maintenant la suite de l'histoire au n° 6.*

5

Félicitations !

→ *Tu peux te rendre au dernier chapitre...*

6

When we arrived at the police station, the police officer who was on night duty* looked really surprised.

"May I ask why teenagers like you aren't in bed at this hour of the night?" he asked.

Betsy burst into tears*. I explained that her twin brother was trapped inside Haunted Manor and that his life was in danger.

"Haunted Manor? But what were you doing in Haunted Manor?"

"Hmm... We were... investigating, sir", I replied.

"Isn't it OUR job to investigate?"

"Yes, it is..."

"So?"

"We were looking for a painting... A painting from the Shipwreck Museum..."

"Are you serious?"

---

on night duty : de garde pour la nuit
burst into tears : éclater en sanglots

"Yes, we are. You can phone Tim Bailey! We saw him this morning. He knows about it."

"Tim Bailey? The old museum director?"

"That's right!"

Betsy was still crying when the police officer started to phone...

Tim Bailey immediately confirmed our story and half an hour later, we were back at the Manor.

A group of policemen began to explore the house while another group disappeared down the tunnel.

Then Betsy and I waited inside one of the police cars. We were so worried about Bill that it was a torture. At last* a policeman knocked at the car window. Bill was next to him...

Bill est-il sain et sauf ?

Pour le savoir, coche la bonne réponse.

1 À quel moment l'officier de police commence-t-il à prendre Ben au sérieux ?

a. Quand Ben lui explique que Bill est retenu prisonnier au manoir et que sa vie est en danger. .... ☐

b. Quand Tim Bailey lui confirme qu'ils sont venus le voir à propos d'un tableau. .... ☐

➡ LIS LE CORRIGÉ N° 2 PAGE 78.

---

at last : enfin

EXPRIMER LA PERMISSION

Dans la question *"May I ask why teenagers like you aren't in bed at this hour of the night?"*, l'officier de police s'adresse à Betsy et Ben :

a. Poliment .... ☐
b. Familièrement .... ☐

Tu as répondu a ➡ VA VOIR LE N° 3.
Tu as répondu b ➡ VA VOIR LE N° 2.

7 

Attention ! Would *est l'auxiliaire du conditionnel. Le futur se construit avec l'auxiliaire* will *suivi de la base verbale.*

→ *Rends-toi au dernier chapitre.*

Corrigés des questions de compréhension

1

1. b. Ben et Betsy entendent une bagarre.
Suddenly we <u>heard</u> the noise of a fight.

2. b. Non, il lui dit qu'il n'ira nulle part.
"YOU are not going anywhere, young man!" the painter replied.

2

1. b. L'officier de police commence à prendre Ben au sérieux quand Tim Bailey lui confirme qu'ils sont venus le voir à propos d'un tableau.
Tim Bailey immediately confirmed our story and half an hour later, we were back at the Manor.

3

1. a. Bill révèle qu'il a retrouvé *Le Naufrage du Stella* parmi d'autres objets de valeur dans le souterrain.
"Did you see "The Wreck of The Stella*" ? Betsy asked." "I did…"*

8

Heroes don't cry!

1

They pushed him into the other car and left immediately in the direction of *Les Nicolles.* That is where criminals are imprisoned on the island.

Now let me explain his business to you: in fact, Chester Fog stored* the things he stole in Haunted Manor until he could sell them on the Internet.

When he stole a painting, he replaced it with a copy. Then he sold the original one to a private collector*.

From time to time, he pretended to sail abroad* for a holiday. In reality, he delivered the goods*.

---

store : stocker
a collector : un collectionneur
abroad : à l'étranger
deliver the goods : livrer la marchandise

Yachting is such a popular pastime on the island that the customs officers* never suspected him.

What about Harold Manson? Well, he never existed! It was the name Chester Fog used when he needed to rent a van... As for Haunted Manor, it was perfect for a trafficker: isolated, linked to the ocean by a secret tunnel and... haunted!
You don't think I'm serious, of course! Well, if you visit Guernsey some day, go to the Manor and see for yourself*!

Cette incroyable affaire est-elle complètement résolue ?

Comment Chester Fog s'y prenait-il pour revendre les objets volés ?

Écris la réponse ci-dessous en français.

C'est ton HUITIÈME INDICE.
N'oublie pas de le noter sur ta page-indices page 95.

LES TOURNURES EXCLAMATIVES

*"Yachting is **such a** popular pastime on the island that the customs officers never suspected him."*

---

customs officers : les inspecteurs des douanes
see for one's self : vérifier

Que veut dire cette phrase ?

a. La navigation de plaisance est un passe-temps **assez** populaire sur l'île et les douaniers ne l'ont jamais soupçonné.
b. La navigation de plaisance est un passe-temps **si** populaire sur l'île **que** les douaniers ne l'ont jamais soupçonné.

Tu as répondu a → VA VOIR LE N° 3.
Tu as répondu b → VA VOIR LE N° 5.

mémo 18

2

Tu t'es trompé(e) ! Le premier verbe de la phrase anglaise est au prétérit, le deuxième au prétérit be + -ing. *Ce deuxième temps signifie que l'action était en cours dans le passé.*

→ *Découvre la fin de l'histoire au n° 4.*

3

C'est une mauvaise réponse ! Dans la phrase proposée, such a popular pastime *est une forme exclamative qui signifie « un passe-temps si populaire ». « Assez populaire » se traduirait par* quite popular.

→ *Lis le n° 5.*

4

It was an invitation to a party at the Shipwreck Museum!
The new director wanted to thank us and celebrate

the return of “The Wreck of *The Stella*”.

For a few days, Bill, Betsy and I felt like heroes! We told our story about a hundred times. It was fun.

And guess what! Our picture was published in the local newspaper. The article was called "Congratulations* to the Three Bees' clan!” (Hmm, thank you, Aunt Sweeny!).

Tim Bailey came to our house when I was packing*.

“I have a present for you”, he said.

It was a book called “The Wreck of *The Stella, Titanic* of the Channel Islands”*.

I was really moved*. In fact, I was on the point of crying.

“Come on, Ben. Heroes don't cry. You know that, don't you?” Tim said.

Then the twins joined us. We had a great afternoon. Finally, they walked me* to the ferryboat... and here I am, waving good-bye to them and

---

congratulations : félicitations
pack : faire ses bagages
“ *The Wreck of* the Stella, Titanic *of the Channel Islands” :* “Le naufrage du *Stella*, le *Titanic* des îles anglo-normandes”
moved : ému
they walked me : ils m'ont accompagné à pied

feeling good about Betsy's SMS on my cell phone...

Of course, you want to know what she wrote to me... But I can't tell you... Unless you have a good reason, it's strictly confidential, you see...

THE END

Bravo! Tu es arrivé(e) à la fin de l'histoire! N'oublie pas de nous envoyer la liste des indices que tu as écrits page 95, sur le site www.lenigme.com : tu pourras télécharger plein de surprises!

À bientôt pour de nouvelles aventures!

5

When we came back to the police-station, Bill and Betsy's parents were waiting for us. They looked extremely angry*.

That is the end of our investigation but not the end of our troubles, I thought…

"Who do you think you are?" they exclaimed. Do you realize how stupid and dangerous it was to play detectives? You risked your lives!

Then Aunt Sweeny and Tim Bailey arrived. Aunt Sweeny was very annoyed too, so Tim Bailey tried to calm everyone down.

"It was my fault… Chester Fog, a trafficker?" I still cannot believe it! I am the one to blame*, I sent these kids to him, he explained.

Finally, we all went home. I was so tired that I slept until three in the afternoon the following day. When I woke up, I had a nice surprise…

angry : en colère
I am the one to blame : c'est à moi qu'il faut vous en prendre

Quelle surprise attend Ben ?

Pour le savoir, coche la bonne réponse.

1 À quoi les trois amis doivent-ils faire face à leur retour au commissariat ?

a. À l'interrogatoire des policiers. . . . . ☐
b. À la colère des parents des jumeaux. . . . . ☐

➡ **LIS LE CORRIGÉ N° 1 PAGE 86.**

LE PRÉTÉRIT PROGRESSIF

Propose la bonne traduction de cette phrase :

"When we came back to the police station, Bill and Betsy's parents were waiting for us."

a. Quand nous sommes rentrés du commissariat de police, les parents de Bill et Betsy nous attendaient.
b. Quand nous rentrons du commissariat de police, les parents de Bill et Betsy sont en train de nous attendre.

Tu as répondu a ➡ VA VOIR LE N° 4.
Tu as répondu b ➡ VA VOIR LE N° 2.

mémo 3

Corrigés des questions de compréhension

1

1. b. Ils doivent faire face à la colère des parents des jumeaux.
Bill and Betsy's parents were waiting for us. They looked extremely angry.

Mémento pour t'aider

Mémento

EXPRIMER L'ABSENCE DE NÉCESSITÉ

1 ***Have to*** + **base verbale** exprime l'idée de nécessité ou d'obligation lorsqu'elle est due aux circonstances.

You have to do your homework! (Tu dois faire tes devoirs !)

Do/Does not have to + **base** verbale exprime l'idée d'absence de nécessité ou d'obligation :

You don't have to go to the haunted manor. (Tu n'es pas obligé d'aller au manoir hanté.)

RACONTER AU PASSÉ

2 **Parler d'une action passée**

Pour parler d'une action passée, on utilise le **prétérit simple** :

I met Bill and Betsy 5 years ago. (J'ai rencontré Bill et Betsy il y a 5 ans.)

Le repère temporel *ago* indique ici le temps écoulé depuis la fin de l'action.

3 **Décrire une action passée**

Pour décrire une action qui était en train de se dérouler dans le passé, on utilise le **prétérit progressif** : il se forme avec ***was*** ou ***were*** suivi de la forme ***-ING***.

I was watching TV when my phone rang. (J'étais en train de regarder la télé quand mon téléphone a sonné.)

EXPRIMER UNE CAPACITÉ OU UNE INCAPACITÉ

4 Les modaux ***can*** et ***could*** sont suivis de l'infinitif sans *to*, ne prennent pas de *-s* à la troisième personne du singulier et se conjuguent sans *do* aux formes interrogatives et négatives.

• ***Can*** exprime la capacité physique et intellectuelle et ***can't*** l'incapacité physique et intellectuelle.

• ***Could*** exprime la capacité au passé et ***couldn't*** l'incapacité au passé. *Could* peut aussi avoir une valeur de conditionnel (souvent utilisé dans les formules de politesse).
Could you come with me, please? (Pourrais-tu venir avec moi s'il te plaît ?)

Exprimer la quantité

5 **Many s'emploie toujours devant un dénombrable** (quelque chose que l'on peut compter)
There are many people on the deck. (Il y a beaucoup de monde sur le pont du bateau.)

Much s'emploie toujours devant un indénombrable (que l'on ne peut pas compter)
There is much wind today. (Il y a beaucoup de vent aujourd'hui.)

L'adjectif qualificatif

6 L'adjectif qualificatif est invariable en anglais et ne peut pas s'accorder avec le nom **ni en nombre ni en genre**. L'adjectif épithète se place devant le nom qu'il qualifie :
A ***white*** yacht. (Un yacht blanc.)

Les questions-tags

7 Elles sont formées d'un auxiliaire et d'un pronom personnel. Lorsque la première partie d'une phrase est à la forme affirmative, le tag est à la forme négative et vice-versa.

*You **are** French, **aren't you**?* (Tu es français n'est-ce pas ?)
*You **are not** French, **are you**?* (Tu n'es pas français, si ?)
S'il n'y a pas d'auxiliaire dans la première partie de la phrase, tu dois utiliser l'auxiliaire du présent ou du prétérit simple : *Do* ou *Does* (présent) / *Did* (passé)
*You like sailing, **don't you**?* (Tu aimes naviguer, n'est ce pas ?)

Exprimer la suggestion

8 L'impératif n'existe qu'à la deuxième personne en anglais et se construit avec l'infinitif sans to : *Look at her!* (Regarde-la !)

Aux autres personnes, on utilise la tournure « ***Let*** **+ complément + infinitif sans *to*** ».
Let's go to the cinema! (Allons au cinéma !)

Mémento

EXPRIMER L'IMPRESSION

9 On peut utiliser différents verbes pour dire « **avoir l'air de** » : *to look, to feel, to sound, to taste, to smell.* Ils peuvent :
- soit être suivis d'un **adjectif** : *She looks sad.* (Elle a l'air triste.)
- soit être **suivis de *like* + nom** : *She looks like her sister.* (Elle ressemble à sa sœur.)

EXPRIMER LA COMPARAISON

10 • Le **comparatif de supériorité** (plus + adjectif + que) :
– Pour un adjectif d'une seule syllabe : **adjectif + er + than.**
She's taller than me. (Elle est plus grande que moi.)
– Pour un adjectif de plus de deux syllabes : **more + adjectif + than.**
This Game cube is more expensive than a traditional game. (Cette Game cube est plus chère qu'un jeu traditionnel.)
• Le **comparatif d'infériorité** (moins + adjectif + que) :
Less* + adjectif de tout type + *than.
He's less clever than his brother. (Il est moins intelligent que son frère.)
• Le **comparatif d'égalité** (aussi + adjectif + que) :
As* + adjectif de tout type + *as.
His house was as messy as his office. (Sa maison était aussi désordonnée que son bureau.)

FAIRE + INFINITIF

11 On forme cette structure grammaticale ainsi :
make* + objet + infinitif sans *to
They made Chester tell the truth. (Ils ont fait dire la vérité à Chester.)

NO ET SES COMPOSÉS

12 On utilise les déterminants ***some, any*** et ***no*** pour quantifier quelque chose.
- ***Some*** s'emploie généralement dans des phrases affirmatives : *I would like some tea please!* (Je voudrais **du** thé.)
- ***Any*** s'emploie généralement dans une phrase interrogative : *I haven't any money left!* (Je n'ai plus d'argent !)
- ***No*** et ***not any*** s'emploient pour exprimer une négation.

Attention ! *No* s'emploie dans les phrases affirmatives tandis que *not any* s'utilise avec une structure négative :
There isn't any tea. (Il n'y a pas de thé.)

Exprimer la probabilité, l'éventualité

13 ***May*** exprime une simple éventualité :
It may rain. (Il se peut qu'il pleuve.)
Might exprime également une éventualité, mais beaucoup moins forte qu'avec *may*.
It might rain tomorrow. (Il se pourrait qu'il pleuve demain.)

Exprimer le conditionnel

14 • Pour s'exprimer au présent ou futur, on utilise **WOULD + base verbale**
I would like to go to the haunted manor with you! (J'aimerais aller au manoir hanté avec toi !)
• Pour s'exprimer au passé, on utilise l'auxiliaire **WOULD + have + participe passé**
I would have liked to go to the haunted manor! (J'aurais aimé aller au manoir hanté !)

Le cas possessif

15 Le cas possessif exprime la **possession** ou la **parenté** et se forme de la façon suivante :
• Au singulier : **Personne ou animal + 's + chose possédée.**
Aunt Sweeny's car (la voiture de tante Sweeny)
• Au pluriel : **Personnes ou animaux + ' + chose possédée**
The boys' bedroom (la chambre des garçons)
Attention ! Certains noms ont un pluriel irrégulier comme *children*, ou *people*. Dans ce cas, on conserve le **'s** du singulier.
The children's hut (la cabane des enfants)

Arrêter de faire quelque chose

16 Pour exprimer le début, la continuation ou la fin d'une action, le verbe doit être suivi de la forme *-ing*. Les verbes pour lesquels on doit appliquer cette règle sont : *begin, start, continue, keep on, go on, stop, quit, finish…*
Stop smoking! (Arrête de fumer !)

Attention ! Ces verbes peuvent être suivis de l'infinitif. Dans ce cas, ils expriment un but.
I stopped to smoke a cigarette. (Je me suis arrêté pour fumer une cigarette.)

S'exprimer au passif

17 Le passif signifie que le sujet subit l'action. On le forme ainsi :
sujet + *be* au temps de la phrase active + verbe au p. passé
The painting represents nine seamen. → Nine seamen are represented in the painting.
Le complément d'agent peut être introduit par ***by***.
Ben offered Betsy flowers. → Betsy was offered flowers by Ben.

Les tournures exclamatives

18 • ***Such*** s'utilise quand l'exclamation porte sur un groupe nominal. Au singulier, *such* est suivi des articles indéfinis ***a*** ou ***an***; au pluriel, il est suivi de l'article **Ø**.
*Ben is **such a** nice boy!* (Ben est un garçon tellement sympa !)
*The 3 B's are **such** nice teenagers!* (Les 3B sont des ados tellement sympas !)
• ***What*** s'emploie soit avec un nom, soit avec un groupe nominal. Il respecte les mêmes règles de construction que *such*.
***What a** beautiful yacht!* (Quel beau yacht !)

Exprimer la durée

19 ***For*** et ***since*** s'emploient pour exprimer une durée.
• **Since** s'emploie lorsque le contenu de la phrase indique un point de départ (un fait précis ou une date).
*I've been in love with Betsy **since 1999**.* (Je suis amoureux de Betsy **depuis 1999**.)
• **For** s'emploie devant une indication de durée (deux heures, six mois…).
*Bill has been missing **for 2 hours**.* (Bill a disparu depuis 2 heures.)

Table des matières

Verbes irréguliers

base verbale	prétérit	participe passé	traduction
be	was *(sing.)* were *(pluriel)*	been	*être*
become	became	become	*devenir*
begin	began	begun	*commencer*
catch	caught	caught	*attraper*
come	came	come	*venir*
do	did	done	*faire*
drive	drove	driven	*conduire*
feel	felt	felt	*(se) sentir*
forget	forgot	forgotten	*oublier*
get	got	got	*aller chercher* get dressed : *s'habiller*
give	gave	given	*donner*
go	went	gone	*aller*
have	had	had	*avoir*
hear	heard	heard	*entendre*
hold	held	held	*tenir*
leave	left	left	*quitter, laisser*
make	made	made	*faire*
meet	met	met	*rencontrer, se retrouver*
put	put	put	*mettre, poser*
run	ran	run	*courir*
say	said	said	*dire*
see	saw	seen	*voir*
sell	sold	sold	*vendre*
send	sent	sent	*envoyer*
show	showed	shown	*montrer*
sit	sat	sat	*s'asseoir*
sleep	slept	slept	*dormir*
steal	stole	stolen	*voler, dérober*
take	took	taken	*prendre*
tell	told	told	*dire*
think	thought	thought	*penser*
wake	woke	woken	wake up : *se réveiller*
write	wrote	written	*écrire*

Page-indices

The Captain is Missing!

de la 5e à la 4^e

Note ci-dessous les indices que tu as trouvés au cours de ta lecture.

Va vite te connecter sur le site

www.lenigme.com

pour nous envoyer tes indices, et tu pourras télécharger plein de

Cadeaux !

Indice 1 : the wreck of the stella

Indice 2 : ....

Indice 3 : ....

Indice 4 : ....

Indice 5 : ....

Indice 6 : ....

Indice 7 : ....

Indice 8 : ....

Bravo ! Tu as trouvé tous les indices !

Tourne la page !

N° d'éditeur : 10175875 - JPMsa - Mars 2011
Imprimé en France par I.M.E. - 25110 Baume-les-Dames

La collection L'ÉNIGME des vacances

Choisis ton univers !

- Historique
- Fantastique
- Policier
- Aventure
- Frisson
- Princesse
- Sciences

du CP au CE1

- Le voleur invisible
- Sophia, princesse de la mer (podcast)
- Le mystère de la source (podcast)

du CE1 au CE2

- La peur au bout de la laisse
- Mystère au cirque Alzared
- Attention ! Dauphins en danger
- Pas si désert que ça !
- Menace sur Madagascar
- Pirates en péril ! (podcast)

du CE2 au CM1

- Le labyrinthe des dragons
- Les fantômes de Glamorgan
- La plage du Prince Blanc
- Le phare de la peur
- Montagne explosive !
- Menaces sur la finale de foot

du CM1 au CM2

- Le voleur de papyrus (iPhone iPad)
- L'œil de feu
- Le sortilège de la pleine lune
- Parfum de vacances
- La carrière interdite
- Feu mystérieux en Australie

du CM2 à la 6e

- Le trésor des Templiers
- Panique à la Pop Academy
- La forêt de l'épouvante
- À la recherche de la cité perdue (iPhone iPad)
- Eaux troubles à Venise

de la 6e à la 5e

- Le secret du Titanic (iPhone iPad)
- Drôle de trafic
- La cinquième fourchette

de la 5e à la 4e

- *Operation Blue Lagoon* (en anglais) (podcast)
- Le saut de l'ange (iPhone iPad)
- *The Captain is Missing!* (en anglais) (podcast)

de la 4e à la 3e

- *Murder in West Park* (en anglais) (podcast)
- *The Mark of the Vampire* (en anglais) (podcast) (iPhone iPad)

(podcast) Histoire à podcaster sur le site www.lenigme.com

iPhone iPad Existe en applications pour iPhone et iPad. Disponible sur App Store.

Retrouve-nous sur le site : www.lenigme.com